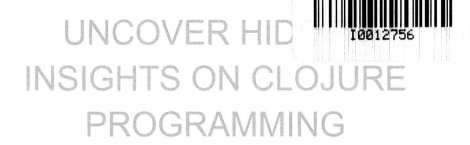

UNCOVER HID   INSIGHTS ON CLOJURE PROGRAMMING

Master SPAs and Dynamic UIs Like a Pro

2024 complete guide

CONTENTS

Preface

Have you ever dreamt of crafting interactive and visually stunning web applications with the power of ClojureScript? This book is your gateway to making that dream a reality!

Whether you're a seasoned web developer or just embarking on your journey, this comprehensive guide empowers you to conquer the exciting realm of Single-Page Applications (SPAs) built with ClojureScript.

Here's a glimpse of what awaits you within these pages:

Solid Foundations: We'll establish a strong understanding of ClojureScript, its core concepts, and its advantages for building SPAs. You'll delve into the fundamentals like data structures, functions, and working with the browser environment using ClojureScript.

Architectural Advantages: Explore the architectural patterns and best practices specifically tailored for crafting robust and maintainable ClojureScript SPAs. Learn how to structure your application for clarity, efficiency, and scalability.

Testing Strategies: Uncover the significance of testing in the SPA development process. We'll equip you with various testing techniques, from unit testing individual components to end-to-end testing the entire user experience. Through effective testing, you'll ensure the quality and reliability of your SPA.

Deployment Dexterity: The book doesn't stop at development. We'll guide you through the deployment process, from selecting the most suitable strategy to utilizing tools like Continuous Integration (CI) pipelines and Content Delivery Networks (CDNs). Learn how to effectively share your masterpiece SPA with the world.

This book is designed to be an interactive companion on your ClojureScript SPA development adventure. The explanations are clear and concise, bolstered by practical examples and code snippets to solidify your understanding. Feel free to experiment with the code samples and put your newfound knowledge into practice.

By the time you reach the final chapter, you'll be equipped with the skills and confidence to construct exceptional ClojureScript SPAs that are not only functional but also performant, secure, and engaging for your users. So, grab your coding tools, buckle up, and get ready to embark on a thrilling journey into the world of

ClojureScript SPA development!

Chapter 1:

Welcome to the World of Clojure

This chapter is your gateway to the exciting world of Clojure development, specifically focusing on building dynamic Single-Page Applications (SPAs) and user interfaces (UIs) like a pro. Whether you're a complete Clojure beginner or have some basic programming experience, this chapter will equip you with the foundation you need to embark on your SPA development journey.

1.1 Why Clojure for Frontend Development?

In the vast landscape of programming languages, Clojure might not be the first name that pops into your head for building frontend experiences. But hold on! Here's why Clojure can be a game-changer for crafting dynamic Single-Page Applications (SPAs) and user interfaces (UIs).

Functional Powerhouse: Clojure embraces a functional programming paradigm. This means you build your application by composing pure functions, leading to:

-Predictable Code: Functions always produce the same output for the same input, making your codebase reliable and easier to test.

-Reduced Side Effects: Functional programming minimizes unexpected behavior and state mutations, often the culprit behind bugs in traditional imperative languages.

-Modular Design: Functions naturally encourage modularity, promoting reusability and maintainability in your SPA components.

Immutable Data Structures: Clojure emphasizes immutability, meaning data remains unchanged after creation. This brings several benefits for frontend development:

-Simplified State Management: Immutable data makes reasoning about application state easier, leading to cleaner and more predictable UIs.

-Concurrent Programming: Clojure's focus on immutability shines in multi-threaded environments, crucial for handling user interactions and updates in SPAs.

-Performance Gains: Immutable data structures enable efficient memory management and optimization for modern web applications.

Lisp Heritage: Clojure, a modern Lisp dialect, leverages the power of Lisp macros. These macros allow you to extend the language itself, creating custom syntax for specific tasks. This can significantly boost your productivity and tailor Clojure to your specific SPA development needs.

JVM Power: Clojure runs on the Java Virtual Machine (JVM), granting access to a vast ecosystem of libraries and tools. You can leverage existing Java libraries for tasks like database interaction, networking, and more, seamlessly integrating them into your Clojure SPAs.

Vibrant Community: The Clojure community is known for its friendliness and helpfulness. If you encounter challenges, you'll find plenty of resources and support available online and at meetups.

By embracing Clojure for frontend development, you gain access to these advantages, potentially leading to cleaner, more maintainable, and performant SPAs. So, are you ready to dive into the exciting world of Clojure and build dynamic web experiences?

1.2 Getting Started with Clojure: Installation and Setup

Now that you're convinced about Clojure's potential for building SPAs, let's get your development environment ready! Here's a step-by-step guide to installing Clojure and setting up your development tools.

Prerequisites:

Java Development Kit (JDK): Clojure runs on the JVM, so you'll need a recent version of the JDK installed on your system. Download and install it from the official Java website: https://www.oracle.com/java/technologies/downloads/.

Text Editor or IDE: While Clojure is flexible with editors, some popular options offer features specifically tailored to Clojure development. Here are a few suggestions:

-Cursive: A powerful Clojure IDE with advanced features like code completion, debugging, and project management.

-Light Table: A lightweight, open-source IDE that supports Clojure development alongside other languages.

-Emacs or Vim: These text editors can be customized with Clojure plugins for syntax highlighting, code navigation, and REPL integration.

Installing Clojure:

There are two primary ways to install Clojure:

-Using the lein installer: Lein is a popular build tool for Clojure projects. Download the appropriate lein installer for your operating system from the official Clojure website: https://clojure.org/guides/install_clojure. Run the downloaded installer script, and it will automatically configure Clojure on your system.

-Downloading the Clojure binary: Download the pre-built Clojure binary distribution from the Clojure website. Extract the downloaded archive and add the path to the `bin` directory containing the `clojure` executable to your system's environment variables.

Verifying Installation:

Once you've installed Clojure, open a terminal window and type `clojure -v`. If the installation was successful, you'll see the installed Clojure version displayed.

Setting Up Your Development Environment:

REPL (Read-Eval-Print Loop): The REPL is a powerful Clojure tool for interactive coding and experimentation. You can interact with Clojure directly in the terminal using the `lein repl` command with lein or launch the REPL within your chosen editor/IDE.

Project Setup (Optional): If you're planning to build a full-fledged SPA, consider using a project management tool like Leiningen or tools.deps to manage dependencies, build tasks, and project structure.

By following these steps, you'll have a functional Clojure development environment ready to tackle your SPA projects. Remember, various resources and tutorials are available online to assist you with specific setup details based on your chosen editor/IDE and project management tool.

1.3 Core Clojure Concepts for Beginners

As you embark on your Clojure journey to build SPAs, grasping some fundamental concepts is crucial. This section will introduce you to the building blocks of Clojure: functions, data structures, and control flow.

1.3.1 Functions: The Heart of Clojure

In Clojure, everything revolves around functions. They are first-class citizens, meaning you can treat them like any other value: assign them to variables, pass them as arguments, and even return them from other functions.

Here's a basic example of a Clojure function that adds two numbers:

Clojure

```
(defn add [x y]
  (+ x y))
```

```
(println (add 5 3)) ; This will print 8
```

1.3.2 Data Structures: Organizing Your Information

Clojure offers a rich set of data structures to hold and manipulate information in your SPA. Here are some commonly used ones:

Numbers: Integers, floating-point numbers, etc.

Strings: Sequences of characters used for text data.

Symbols: Unique identifiers representing keywords or concepts.

Lists: Ordered collections of elements, enclosed in parentheses `( )`.

Vectors: Similar to lists, but offer faster random access by index.

Maps: Unordered collections of key-value pairs enclosed in curly braces `{ }`.

1.3.3 Control Flow: Directing the Execution

Control flow statements dictate how your program executes code based on certain conditions. Here are some essential control flow elements in Clojure:

if statements: Evaluate a condition and execute code based on the result (true or false).

cond statements: Similar to if statements but allow checking multiple conditions at once.

loops: Iterate through collections or repeat actions a specific number of times.

`-do`: Executes a sequence of expressions.

`- for`: Iterates over a collection and executes code for each element.

`- while`: Repeats a block of code as long as a condition is true.

Learning Resources:

While this section provides a brief overview, plenty of resources can deepen your understanding of these core Clojure concepts. Consider exploring the official Clojure documentation (https://clojure.org/) and online tutorials specifically geared towards beginners.

By mastering these fundamentals, you'll be well-equipped to build the foundation for your dynamic SPAs in Clojure.

1.4 Setting Up Your Clojure Development Environment

Now that you've grasped the core concepts of Clojure, it's time to craft your development environment – your personal playground for building amazing SPAs. This section will guide you through choosing the right tools and configuring them for a smooth Clojure development experience.

Choosing Your Editor/IDE:

While Clojure can work with any text editor, some offer features specifically tailored to the language, making your development process more efficient. Here are some popular options to consider:

Cursive: A powerful Clojure IDE with features like:

-Code completion for functions, variables, and keywords

-Debugging tools to pinpoint errors in your code

-Project management capabilities to organize your SPA codebase

-REPL integration for interactive Clojure experimentation within the IDE

Light Table: A lightweight, open-source IDE that supports Clojure alongside other languages. It offers:

-Syntax highlighting for Clojure code

-Code folding to hide or expand code sections for better readability

-REPL integration for interactive evaluation of Clojure expressions

Emacs or Vim: These powerful text editors can be customized with Clojure plugins providing:

-Syntax highlighting for Clojure code

-Parenthesis matching and indentation assistance

-REPL integration through plugins like Cider for Emacs or Parinfer for Vim

The REPL (Read-Eval-Print Loop):

The REPL is an essential tool for interactive Clojure development. It allows you to enter Clojure expressions directly in the terminal or your editor's integrated REPL, evaluate them, and see the results immediately. This is a fantastic way to experiment with code snippets, test functions, and learn Clojure interactively.

Launching the REPL:

The method for launching the REPL depends on your chosen setup:

Leiningen: Use the `lein repl` command in your terminal to start a REPL connected to your current project.

Standalone Clojure: Run the `clojure` executable in your terminal to launch a general REPL.

Editor/IDE Plugins: Most Clojure-friendly editors/IDEs offer integrated REPLs accessible through their interfaces.

Project Management (Optional):

For larger SPA projects, consider using a project management tool like Leiningen or tools.deps. These tools help you manage dependencies (libraries your project relies on), automate build tasks (compiling and packaging your SPA code), and maintain a clean project structure.

Customizing Your Environment:

Once you've chosen your tools, explore their settings and customization options. Here are some aspects you might want to adjust:

Keyboard Shortcuts: Configure keyboard shortcuts for frequently used actions like running the REPL, saving files, or code formatting.

Themes: Select a theme that suits your preferences for better code readability and a visually appealing development environment.

Linters and Formatters: Consider integrating linters that check your code for errors and formatters that enforce consistent code style for improved maintainability.

Learning Resources:

The official Clojure documentation (https://clojure.org/) provides detailed guides on setting up a Clojure development environment. Additionally, numerous online tutorials and resources showcase specific editor/IDE configurations for Clojure development.

By following these steps and exploring customization options, you'll create a comfortable and efficient development environment tailored to your needs – a perfect launchpad for building dynamic SPAs with Clojure!

Chapter 2:

Unveiling the Power of Single-Page Applications (SPAs)

In today's fast-paced web landscape, Single-Page Applications (SPAs) have revolutionized user experiences. This chapter delves into the world of SPAs, exploring their core concepts, the advantages they offer when built with Clojure, and the challenges you might encounter along the way.

2.1 Understanding the SPA Architecture

Traditional web applications function like a flipbook. Every time you interact with the page, like clicking a button or submitting a form, the entire page reloads from the server. This can lead to a clunky and slow user experience.

Single-Page Applications (SPAs) take a different approach. Here's a breakdown of the SPA architecture that will transform how you build web applications:

Single HTML Document: Imagine the foundation of your house. In an SPA, this foundation is a single HTML document loaded initially. This document acts as the skeleton of your entire application.

Dynamic Content: Instead of reloading the whole page, SPAs update specific sections of the content using JavaScript. Think of replacing a single brick in your house wall – much faster and smoother than rebuilding the entire structure!

Client-Side Rendering: A significant part of the magic happens on the user's browser using JavaScript frameworks like React or

Angular. These frameworks are like skilled construction workers, efficiently rendering the UI (user interface) elements within the single HTML document.

API Communication: SPAs don't operate in isolation. They communicate with backend servers using APIs (Application Programming Interfaces) to fetch and update data as needed. Imagine APIs as delivery trucks bringing necessary supplies (data) to your construction site (SPA).

2.2 Benefits of Building SPAs with Clojure: A Functional Edge

While you can build SPAs with various languages, Clojure offers some unique advantages that stem from its functional programming approach. Here's how Clojure empowers you to create robust, efficient, and maintainable SPAs:

Clean and Predictable Code: Functional programming emphasizes clear functions that take inputs and produce consistent outputs. This leads to code that's easier to understand, test, and debug – a critical factor for managing the complexity of SPAs. Imagine your SPA code as a well-organized toolbox; with Clojure, every tool (function) has a designated place and behaves predictably, making development smoother.

Taming State Management: One of the biggest challenges in SPAs is managing application state – essentially, keeping track of all the data that affects what the user sees on the screen. Clojure's focus on immutable data structures simplifies this process. Since data doesn't change after creation, reasoning about its state becomes more manageable, leading to predictable and stable UI behavior in your SPA. Think of immutable data structures like building blocks that lock into place once assembled, ensuring the overall structure (your SPA's UI) remains stable.

Boosting Productivity with Macros: Clojure's Lisp heritage comes with a superpower – macros. These macros allow you to extend the language itself by creating custom syntax for repetitive tasks in SPA development. Imagine macros as pre-assembled code snippets you can reuse throughout your SPA. This saves you time and effort, letting you focus on the unique aspects of your application.

Seamless ClojureScript Integration: SPAs heavily rely on JavaScript for client-side functionality. ClojureScript, a dialect of Clojure that compiles to JavaScript, bridges the gap. You can leverage existing ClojureScript libraries specifically designed for building SPAs, like Om or Reagent. These libraries integrate seamlessly with your Clojure backend, allowing you to write most of your application logic in the familiar Clojure environment.

Standing on the Shoulders of Giants: The Clojure community is renowned for its helpfulness. If you encounter challenges while building your SPA, you'll find a wealth of online resources, tutorials, and forums filled with knowledgeable Clojure developers ready to assist you. Consider the Clojure community your supportive team of construction workers – always there to help you navigate the development process and overcome hurdles.

By harnessing these advantages, Clojure empowers you to build SPAs that are not only functional but also clean, maintainable, and performant – a perfect foundation for exceptional web applications.

2.3 Common Challenges of SPAs and How Clojure Helps

Building dynamic and interactive SPAs comes with its own set of hurdles. Here's a closer look at some common challenges you might encounter and how Clojure's functional approach can help you overcome them:

Challenge: Client-Side Complexity

The Problem: As your SPA grows, managing complex logic on the user's browser can become overwhelming. Traditional imperative programming can lead to tangled code that's difficult to reason about and maintain.

Clojure's Solution: Clojure's functional paradigm promotes code modularity and reusability. You break down complex logic into smaller, well-defined functions. These functions are easier to understand, test, and reuse in different parts of your SPA, reducing overall complexity. Imagine building your SPA with LEGO bricks – each brick (function) has a specific purpose and can be combined in various ways to create intricate structures without chaos.

Challenge: State Management

The Problem: Keeping track of application state across various UI components in an SPA can be tricky. Inconsistent or unpredictable state can lead to unexpected behavior and a frustrating user experience.

Clojure's Solution: Clojure's emphasis on immutability simplifies state management. Data structures are immutable, meaning they can't be changed after creation. This makes reasoning about application state significantly easier. Instead of constantly worrying about data mutations, you can focus on creating new states derived from the old ones, leading to more predictable and stable UI behavior in your SPA. Think of state management in Clojure like a recipe – you start with a set of ingredients (initial state) and follow clear instructions (functions) to transform them into new dishes (updated states) without altering the original ingredients.

Challenge: Performance Optimization

The Problem: A sluggish SPA can lead to frustrated users and a negative perception of your application. Ensuring smooth performance requires efficient code that avoids unnecessary processing.

Clojure's Solution: Clojure's focus on immutability and lazy evaluation contributes to optimized performance in SPAs. Lazy evaluation means calculations are performed only when necessary. This avoids unnecessary processing of unused data, improving the overall efficiency of your SPA. Imagine lazy evaluation like a smart grocery shopper who only buys what they need – your SPA code only processes data when it's required for the UI, avoiding unnecessary computations that could slow things down.

By understanding these challenges and leveraging Clojure's strengths, you can build SPAs that are not only functional but also robust, maintainable, and performant, providing a delightful user experience.

2.4 Real-World Examples of SPAs Built with Clojure

Several real-world applications demonstrate the power of Clojure for building SPAs. Here are a few examples to inspire you:

Commute: A collaborative workspace platform built with ClojureScript, offering a dynamic and responsive user interface.

Datomic:A powerful database platform that utilizes Clojure for its web interface, showcasing efficient data management within an SPA.

Light Table: The previously mentioned lightweight IDE itself is an SPA built with Clojure, demonstrating its capabilities for building interactive developer tools.

Exploring these examples can provide valuable insights and inspiration for your own SPA development journey with Clojure. By leveraging Clojure's functional approach, you can create clean, maintainable, and performant SPAs that offer exceptional user experiences.

Chapter 3:

Laying the Foundation: Building Your First Clojure SPA

Congratulations! You've grasped the core concepts of Clojure and unlocked the potential of SPAs. Now it's time to dive into the exciting world of building your first Clojure SPA. This chapter will guide you through the essential steps to get your SPA up and running.

3.1 Project Setup and Essential Libraries: Gearing Up for Your First Clojure SPA

Now that you're excited to build your first Clojure SPA, let's gather the necessary tools and libraries to set the stage for your development journey.

Essential Ingredients:

Clojure Development Environment: Make sure you have Clojure installed and your chosen editor/IDE configured as described in Chapter 1.4. A well-configured environment will streamline your development process.

Project Management (Optional): While not mandatory, using a project management tool like Leiningen can significantly simplify your life, especially for larger SPAs. Leiningen helps you manage dependencies (libraries your project relies on), automate build tasks (compiling and packaging your SPA code), and maintain a clean project structure. If you're new to Clojure projects, consider using Leiningen – it can save you time and effort in the long run.

Building Blocks for Your SPA:

Here are some essential ClojureScript libraries you'll likely encounter when building SPAs:

Reagent: A popular library that simplifies creating reusable Clojure components for building dynamic user interfaces in your SPA. Think of Reagent as a toolbox filled with pre-built UI elements you can assemble to create your SPA's interface.

Om Next: Another option for building user interfaces with ClojureScript. Om Next offers a more functional approach compared to Reagent. If you're comfortable with a functional style, Om Next might be a good choice for you.

React/React-dom: If you're already familiar with React, you can leverage React libraries alongside ClojureScript for SPA development. This allows you to use your existing React knowledge while benefiting from Clojure's functional programming power in your backend logic.

Choosing Your Library:

The choice between these libraries depends on your preferences and project requirements. Here's a quick breakdown to help you decide:

Reagent: A good starting point for beginners due to its approachable syntax and focus on reusability.

Om Next: Ideal for those who prefer a more functional approach and want tighter integration with Clojure concepts.

React/React-dom: A powerful option if you're already familiar with React and its ecosystem.

Project Structure with Leiningen (Optional):

If you choose to use Leiningen, it provides a convenient default project structure. You can create a new Leiningen project specifically for your SPA using the `lein new [project-name] spa` command. This creates a well-organized directory layout for your code, resources, and configuration files, making it easier to manage your project as it grows.

By having the right tools and libraries in place, you'll be well-equipped to embark on your Clojure SPA development adventure. In the next section, we'll delve into creating a basic user interface using Hiccup, the syntax for describing HTML structures within Clojure.

3.2 Creating a Basic User Interface with Hiccup: Building the Blocks of Your SPA

Now that you have your project set up with the necessary tools, let's begin constructing the foundation of your SPA – the user interface (UI). We'll use Hiccup, a powerful tool for describing HTML elements within Clojure.

Hiccup: Your SPA's Building Blocks

Imagine Hiccup as a set of Lego bricks for building your SPA's UI. Each Hiccup expression represents an HTML element, allowing you to create familiar components like headings, paragraphs, buttons, and more. Here's an example:

Clojure

```
(defn hello-world []

  [:h1 "Welcome to Your First Clojure SPA!"])
```

This code defines a function named `hello-world` that returns a vector representing an HTML `h1` element with the text "Welcome to Your First Clojure SPA!". This vector can be used by Reagent or other UI libraries to render the actual heading element on the screen.

Breaking Down the Hiccup Syntax:

`(defn hello-world [] ...)`: This defines a function named `hello-world` that takes no arguments (`[]`).

`[:h1 "Welcome to Your First Clojure SPA!"]`: This is the Hiccup expression that represents the `h1` element.

> `:h1`: This specifies the HTML element type – in this case, an `h1` heading.

> `"Welcome to Your First Clojure SPA!"`: The text content that will be displayed within the heading element.

Rendering the UI with Reagent:

Hiccup provides the building blocks, but to display them on the screen, you'll need a UI library like Reagent. Here's how you can render the `hello-world` component within your main application setup using Reagent:

Clojure

```clojure
(defn main []

  (reagent/render (hello-world) (.getElementById
js/document "app")))
```

This code defines a `main` function that uses `reagent/render` to render the `hello-world` component element. The second argument, `.getElementById js/document "app"`, specifies the DOM element in your HTML document where the component should be displayed. The `getElementById` function fetches the element with the ID "app" from the HTML document, and `reagent/render` takes care of injecting the UI elements created from your Hiccup expressions into that DOM element.

With this basic understanding of Hiccup and Reagent working together, you can start creating more complex UIs for your SPA. In the next section, we'll explore how to add interactivity to your UI using events and state management.

3.3 Handling User Interaction and Events: Breathing Life into Your Clojure SPA

A static UI might be informative, but true SPAs shine with interactivity. This section dives into how you can handle user interactions and events in your Clojure SPA, making it dynamic and responsive.

Making Your SPA Reactive: Events and Handlers

Imagine your SPA as a conversation. Users interact with your UI elements (like buttons), triggering events that your application needs to respond to. Here's how to create event handlers in Clojure:

Clojure

```
(defn hello-world []
  (let [text-atom (atom "Welcome")]
    [:div
      [:h1 @text-atom]
```

```
    [:button {:on-click #(swap! text-atom #(str
"Clicked! " %))} "Click Me!"]]))
```

This code introduces a few key concepts for handling user interaction:

atom: We use atom from Clojure's core library to manage the application state. In this case, the state is the current text displayed in the heading. An atom is a mutable reference that holds the state value.

Event Handler: The button element has an :on-click key. This key defines an event handler function that gets executed when the button is clicked.

Updating State: The event handler function uses swap! to update the value stored in the text-atom. swap! takes a function that receives the current state value and returns the updated value. In this case, the function prepends "Clicked! " to the existing text, effectively updating the application state based on the user interaction.

With this approach, clicking the button triggers the event handler, updates the state (text content), and re-renders the UI with the modified text, providing a dynamic user experience.

Common Event Handlers:

Here are some other commonly used event handlers in Clojure SPAs:

:on-change: Used for input elements like text fields or select boxes to capture user input and update the state accordingly.

`:on-submit`: Typically used for forms to handle form submissions and perform necessary actions.

`:on-key-down`: Useful for capturing keyboard events, such as enabling functionality based on specific key presses.

By leveraging these event handlers and state management techniques, you can create SPAs that respond to user interactions and provide a seamless user experience. In the next section, we'll explore how to handle routing in your SPA, allowing users to navigate between different views or pages within your application.

3.4 Routing Fundamentals in Your Clojure SPA: Navigating Your Application

As your SPA grows, you'll likely want to display different content based on the URL. Users expect to be able to navigate between different sections of your application seamlessly. This section provides a foundational understanding of routing in Clojure SPAs.

The Road Map of Your SPA: Routing Concepts

Imagine your SPA as a city with various districts (views or pages). Routing helps users navigate between these districts by understanding the URL structure and displaying the corresponding content. Here's a glimpse into routing with Reagent:

Clojure

```clojure
(defn about-page []
  [:div "This is the About page!"])

(defn navigate! [page]
  (set! (.-hash js/location) (str "#" page)))

(defn main []
```

```
(let [page (when-some (.-hash js/location)
(subs (.-hash js/location) 1))]
  (if (= page "about")
    (about-page)
    (hello-world))))
```

This code introduces a basic routing mechanism:

about-page **Function:** This function defines the content for the "About" page of your SPA.

navigate! **Function:** This function allows you to programmatically change the URL fragment (the part after the hash symbol #). It takes a page name as input and updates the URL hash accordingly.

Routing Logic in main**:** The main function checks the current URL fragment using (.-hash js/location). If a fragment exists, it extracts the page name using (subs (.-hash js/location) 1). The code then conditionally renders either the hello-world component (for the root path) or the about-page component based on the presence and value of the URL fragment.

Building a More Robust Routing System:

While this is a simplified example, more complex SPAs often use dedicated routing libraries for features like:

Defining routes and their associated components.

Matching the current URL to a specific route.

Handling parameters within URLs.

Providing features like navigation history and transitions between views.

Some popular routing libraries for Clojure SPAs include:

```
re-router
fulcroot
```

These libraries offer more advanced functionalities to manage routing in your SPAs as they grow in complexity.

By understanding the basics of routing and exploring available libraries, you can ensure a smooth and intuitive navigation experience for users within your Clojure SPA.

In the next chapter, we'll delve deeper into data fetching and handling asynchronous operations in your Clojure SPA, essential aspects for building dynamic and interactive web applications.

Chapter 4:

Mastering Dynamic Data Management in SPAs

Congratulations! You've built the foundation for your Clojure SPA. Now, let's explore how to manage data effectively, a crucial aspect of creating dynamic and interactive web applications. This chapter dives into data fetching, handling asynchronous operations, and techniques for keeping your SPA's UI in sync with the underlying data.

4.1 Data Fetching Strategies: Fueling Your SPA

Imagine your SPA as a bustling restaurant. To prepare delicious dishes (user interfaces) for your guests, you need fresh ingredients – data – delivered from reliable sources. Data fetching is the process of retrieving data from external sources, like servers or APIs (Application Programming Interfaces), that act as your kitchen suppliers. Here are some common data fetching strategies you can use to keep your Clojure SPA running smoothly:

Manual Fetching with `fetch`: For a hands-on approach, you can leverage the built-in `fetch` function in ClojureScript. This function allows you to make HTTP requests directly to APIs, giving you fine-grained control over the fetching process. However, this approach can become tedious and complex for managing multiple API interactions and keeping your UI components up-to-date.

Libraries for Asynchronous Data Fetching: To simplify your life and streamline data fetching, consider using established ClojureScript libraries. These libraries encapsulate the complexities of asynchronous operations and data handling, providing a more convenient and declarative approach:

`re-fetch`: This lightweight library is a popular choice for its simplicity and focus on declarative data fetching. You define how to fetch data, and `re-fetch` handles the underlying asynchronous operations and automatically updates your UI components when the data arrives.

`re-com`: A more comprehensive library, `re-com` not only handles data fetching but also provides features for state management and component composition. It offers a structured approach to building UIs and managing data flow in your SPA.

`Om Next`: As mentioned earlier, Om Next, another popular library for building ClojureScript SPAs, has built-in mechanisms for fetching data from external sources and keeping your UI components synchronized with the latest information.

These libraries often leverage core Clojure features like `core.async` and channels to manage asynchronous operations efficiently. By using these libraries, you can focus on the core logic of your application while ensuring smooth data fetching and UI updates.

4.2 Handling Asynchronous Operations: Keeping Your SPA Responsive

In the world of SPAs, data fetching often involves asynchronous operations. This means your application code might continue executing while waiting for data to arrive from an API or other external source. Imagine your SPA as a waiter taking an order – they can't wait around for the food to be cooked before taking new orders from other customers. Similarly, your SPA shouldn't freeze up while waiting for data. It's crucial to handle these asynchronous operations effectively to prevent a sluggish or unresponsive user experience.

Here's how Clojure shines in handling asynchronous operations:

Immutability: A core principle in Clojure, immutability simplifies reasoning about application state during asynchronous operations. Since you don't mutate existing data, but rather create new data structures representing the updated state, it becomes easier to predict how your UI should behave based on the incoming data.

Core.async and Channels: Clojure's `core.async` library provides powerful tools for managing asynchronous operations efficiently. Channels act like message queues, allowing you to send and receive data asynchronously without blocking your main application thread. Think of channels as a designated waiting area for incoming data – messages are delivered there without interrupting your main application flow. This ensures a smooth user experience for your SPA users, even while data is being fetched in the background.

Libraries for Managing Async Flow: Data fetching libraries for ClojureScript often build upon `core.async`. They provide abstractions and patterns specifically designed for managing the flow of data in your SPA. These libraries handle tasks like making API requests, receiving responses, and updating the UI accordingly, freeing you from writing complex asynchronous code yourself.

By understanding these concepts and leveraging the available tools, you can build SPAs that are not only functional but also responsive and user-friendly, even when dealing with asynchronous data operations. In the next section, we'll explore techniques for keeping your UI components in sync with the underlying data, ensuring your SPA reflects the latest information.

4.3 Error Handling and Optimistic Updates: Making Your SPA Robust

Even the most meticulously crafted SPAs can encounter errors during data fetching. Here's how to make your Clojure SPA resilient and user-friendly in the face of unexpected situations:

Error Handling: Implement proper error handling mechanisms to gracefully handle situations where data fetching fails. Imagine your SPA encountering a kitchen mishap – you don't want your guests to be left hanging! Here's what you can do:

-Informative Error Messages: Display clear and informative error messages to the user, explaining the issue and potential next steps. This helps users understand what went wrong and prevents frustration.

-Retry Logic: In some cases, you might want to implement retry logic for failed requests. This could involve retrying after a short delay or providing a button for the user to manually retry the operation.

+Fallback Data: Consider having fallback data or a default state to display in case the main data fetch fails. This ensures your UI doesn't become completely blank and provides a basic level of functionality while you handle the error.

Optimistic Updates: To improve the perceived performance of your SPA, you might consider optimistic updates. This means:

-Simulating Success: While data is being fetched, temporarily update the UI to reflect the anticipated data. This can give users the impression of a faster response time, as they see the UI update immediately.

-Handling Inconsistencies: Be prepared to handle potential inconsistencies if the data fetch ultimately fails. You might need to revert the optimistic update and display an error message to the user.

By incorporating these practices, you can ensure that your SPA remains informative and user-friendly even when unexpected errors arise. Imagine your restaurant kitchen having a backup plan in case an order encounters a problem – optimistic updates allow you to provide a smooth initial experience while having fail-safes in place.

The next section, 4.4 Beyond the Basics: Advanced Data Management Techniques, will explore some additional strategies for handling complex data scenarios in your Clojure SPA.

4.4 Beyond the Basics: Advanced Data Management Techniques

As your Clojure SPA grows and handles more complex data interactions, you might explore some advanced data management techniques to optimize performance and user experience. Here are a few examples:

Client-Side Caching: Imagine your restaurant having a pantry to store frequently used ingredients – client-side caching works similarly. By caching frequently accessed data on the user's browser, you can reduce the number of API calls required for subsequent visits to the same data. This can significantly improve the perceived performance of your SPA, especially for users with slow or unreliable internet connections.

Pagination and Infinite Scrolling: For very large datasets that could overwhelm users with a massive initial load, consider implementing pagination or infinite scrolling.

-Pagination: This technique divides the data into smaller, manageable pages. Users can navigate between pages to view different portions of the dataset. This approach is suitable for situations where users don't necessarily need to see the entire dataset at once.

-Infinite Scrolling: As users scroll down the page, new data chunks are automatically fetched and appended to the existing content. This creates a seamless user experience for exploring large datasets without needing manual pagination.

-Both pagination and infinite scrolling require careful implementation to ensure smooth loading, efficient data management, and a clear visual indication to the user of how much data has been loaded and whether more is available.

Offline Functionality: In an ideal world, your SPA would always have an internet connection. However, providing some level of offline functionality can enhance user experience. This might involve storing essential data locally within the browser's storage mechanisms and using it to display a limited but functional UI even when offline. You can then synchronize the local data with the server whenever the user regains internet connectivity.

By exploring these advanced techniques and choosing the ones that best suit your specific SPA's needs, you can create a robust and user-friendly data management system for your application. Remember, the key is to find the right balance between performance, user experience, and data consistency for your unique SPA requirements.

This concludes Chapter 4 on Mastering Dynamic Data Management in SPAs. The following chapters will delve into other aspects of building effective Clojure SPAs.

Chapter 5:

Building Interactive UIs with ClojureScript

Congratulations! You've grasped the fundamentals of data fetching and keeping your SPA's UI in sync with the underlying data. Now, let's dive into the heart of a user's experience – crafting interactive user interfaces (UIs) with ClojureScript. This chapter explores essential concepts and techniques for building dynamic and engaging UIs for your Clojure SPA.

5.1 Component-Based Architecture: The Foundation of Your SPA's UI

Imagine your SPA's user interface (UI) as a beautiful house. To construct this house, you wouldn't build it all in one go – instead, you'd break it down into manageable sections like walls, doors, and windows. Component-based architecture adopts a similar approach for building SPAs. It's a popular strategy where you decompose the UI into reusable components, each with a specific function.

Here are some key benefits of using a component-based architecture:

Reusability: Components can be reused throughout your SPA, reducing the amount of code you need to write and maintain. Imagine if you could reuse the same door design throughout the house – that's the beauty of reusable components!

Modularity: Complex UIs can be broken down into smaller, more manageable components. This improves the organization and readability of your codebase. Just like a well-organized house is easier to navigate, modular components make your SPA easier to understand and modify.

Testability: Isolated components are much easier to test in unit isolation. This leads to more robust and reliable UIs, ensuring each building block functions as intended before assembling the entire house (SPA).

In essence, component-based architecture promotes a structured and efficient way to build complex and maintainable SPAs. The next section will delve into popular UI libraries for ClojureScript that can help you implement this approach in your projects.

5.2 Popular UI Libraries for ClojureScript: Choosing the Right Tool for the Job

In Chapter 5.1, we explored the concept of component-based architecture for building SPAs in ClojureScript. Now, let's delve into specific libraries that can help you implement this approach and create interactive UIs. Here are some of the most popular options:

Reagent:

Focus: Simplicity and Declarative Style

Key Features:

-Leverages React's virtual DOM for efficient UI updates.

- Declarative approach – you describe what the UI should look like, and Reagent handles the updates.

-Popular choice for beginners due to its approachable syntax.

Om Next:

Focus: Functional Approach

Key Features:

-Integrates well with core Clojure concepts for a functional programming experience.

-Provides a more functional approach to building UI components compared to Reagent.

-Offers features for handling subscriptions and managing application state.

Re-frame:

Focus: Application Architecture and Separation of Concerns

Key Features:

-Encourages a clear separation of concerns between UI components, business logic, and data management through subscriptions.

-Provides a structured approach for building complex SPAs.

-Might have a steeper learning curve compared to Reagent for beginners.

Choosing the right library depends on several factors:

-Your Preferences: Do you prefer a declarative or functional style of programming?

-Project Requirements: Consider the complexity of your SPA and the features you need.

-Familiarity: If you're already familiar with React or functional programming concepts, you might have a preference for Reagent or Om Next, respectively.

Here's a table summarizing the key points:

Library	Focus	Key Features	Suitable for
Reagent	Simplicity, Declarative	Virtual DOM, Declarative approach, Easy to learn	Beginners, UIs with frequent updates
Om Next	Functional Approach	Integrates with Clojure concepts, Functional components, Subscriptions	Functional programmers, Complex SPAs

| Re-frame | Application Architecture | Separation of concerns, Subscriptions, Structured approach | Complex SPAs, Well-defined application architecture |

Remember, these are just a few of the many ClojureScript UI libraries available. Don't hesitate to explore other options that might better suit your specific needs. In the next section, we'll dive deeper into the core concepts involved in building UI components with ClojureScript.

5.3 The Building Blocks of Your SPA: Core Concepts in UI Component Construction

Now that you've explored the advantages of component-based architecture and popular UI libraries in ClojureScript, let's delve into the essential concepts involved in building those UI components. Here are the fundamentals you'll need to understand:

Component Functions:

Imagine a blueprint for a house component. In ClojureScript, UI components are typically defined as functions. These functions take two main arguments:

-Input Data (props): This data provides information to the component about what to display and how to behave. Think of props as instructions passed to a builder specifying how to construct a particular component of the house (UI). Props are usually immutable data structures like maps or vectors.

-Returns Hiccup Structures: The component function returns a Hiccup structure representing the HTML elements that make up the component's UI. Hiccup is a powerful tool in ClojureScript for describing HTML elements in a Clojure-friendly way.

Props: The Instructions for Your Components

As mentioned earlier, props are immutable data structures that provide instructions to components. They determine what the component will display and how it will interact with the user. Here's an analogy:

-Imagine building a door component. A prop named `color` might be set to `"red"` to instruct the component to render a red door. Another prop named `handle-type` could be set to `"knob"` or `"handle-less"` to specify the type of handle the door should have.

-Props allow for creating flexible and reusable components that can adapt their behavior based on the data they receive.

Component Lifecycle: When Your Components Come and Go

Some UI libraries, like Reagent and Om Next, offer lifecycle methods for components. These methods allow you to perform actions at specific stages of a component's existence, similar to the lifecycle of a building component being constructed, used, and eventually removed. Here are some examples of lifecycle methods:

`on-mount`: This method is called when the component is first inserted into the UI, similar to when a new house component is built and installed. You can use this method to fetch data or perform other initialization tasks.

`on-update`: This method is called whenever the component receives new props, akin to renovating a house component with a fresh coat of paint (updated props). You can use this method to update the component's UI based on the new data.

`on-unmount`: This method is called when the component is removed from the UI, similar to removing a house component during demolition. You can use this method to clean up any resources associated with the component.

By understanding these core concepts, you'll be well-equipped to construct reusable and dynamic UI components for your ClojureScript SPAs. The next section, 5.4 Building Interactive Components with Events, will explore how to make your components respond to user interactions, adding life to your SPA's UI.

5.4 Bringing Your UI to Life: Building Interactive Components with Events

A static user interface might be informative, but true engagement comes from interactivity. In this section, we'll explore how to create event handlers in your ClojureScript components to make them respond to user interactions. This is what truly transforms your SPA from a brochure into a dynamic and engaging application.

Here's an example of a simple counter component that utilizes an event handler:

Clojure

```clojure
(defn counter [count]
  [:div
    [:h2 "Count: " count]
      [:button {:on-click #(swap! count inc)}
"Increment"]])
```

Deconstructing the Code:

-This code defines a `counter` component that takes a `count` value as input.

-The component displays the current count value and an "Increment" button.

-The key element here is the button. It has a key named `:on-click` that defines an event handler function.

-When the button is clicked, the event handler function is executed. This function utilizes `swap!` to update the `count` atom, effectively increasing the count displayed by the component.

Event Handlers: The Bridge Between User and UI

-Event handlers are functions that are associated with specific events, like button clicks or form submissions. When the event occurs (e.g., button clicked), the corresponding event handler is triggered.

-In our example, the `:on-click` event handler is triggered when the button is clicked. This allows the component to react to user interaction and update its UI accordingly.

Common Event Handlers in SPAs

-Here are some other commonly used event handlers in ClojureScript SPAs:

`:on-change`: Used for input elements like text fields or select boxes to capture user input and update the component's state accordingly.

`:on-submit`: Typically used for forms to handle form submissions and perform necessary actions within your application logic.

`:on-key-down`: Useful for capturing keyboard events, such as enabling functionality based on specific key presses (e.g., search functionality with the Enter key).

By leveraging event handlers and keeping your component's state updated, you can create interactive UI components that respond to user actions, providing a more engaging and dynamic user experience for your ClojureScript SPA.

The next section, 5.5 Handling Form Interactions and User Input, will delve deeper into how to create interactive forms and handle user input within your SPA's components.

5.5 Capturing User Input: Forms and Interactions in Your SPA

Forms are essential elements in SPAs, allowing users to provide input and interact with your application. In this section, we'll explore how to create interactive forms and handle user input within your ClojureScript components.

Here's an example of a basic form component that captures user input and calls a provided function on submission:

Clojure

```
(defn todo-form [on-submit]
  [:form {:on-submit on-submit}
      [:input {:type "text" :placeholder "Add a
todo"}]
    [:button "Add"]])
```

Building the Form Component:

-This code defines a `todo-form` component that takes an `on-submit` function as input.

-The form element itself has an `:on-submit` event handler that calls the provided `on-submit` function when the form is submitted (typically when the user clicks the "Add" button).

-Within the form, an input field allows users to enter their todo item.

Capturing User Input with Event Handlers:

-The `:on-submit` event handler plays a crucial role here. When the user submits the form (clicks the button), this event handler is triggered.

-Inside the event handler function, you can access the user's input from the form fields. Libraries like Reagent provide mechanisms to extract this data and use it within your application logic.

Utilizing the Captured Input:

-The `on-submit` function passed as a prop allows you to define the behavior when the form is submitted. This function can be responsible for various actions, such as:

Adding the new todo item to a list maintained by your application state.

Sending the data to your server-side API for further processing.

Performing any necessary validation on the user input before proceeding.

By understanding how to create forms and handle user input within your components, you can build SPAs that allow users to interact with your application and provide valuable data.

This concludes the exploration of Chapter 5: Building Interactive UIs with ClojureScript. The next chapters will delve into other aspects of building effective ClojureScript SPAs.

Chapter 6:

Conquering User Interface Complexity with Component-Building Design

As your ClojureScript SPA grows in features and functionality, managing the UI complexity can become a challenge. This chapter explores the concept of component-based design (CBD) as a powerful approach to structure and maintain complex UIs.

6.1 Keeping Your House in Order: The Challenge of UI Complexity in SPAs

Imagine a beautiful house that starts out neat and organized. But as you accumulate more furniture, decorations, and belongings, things can quickly become cluttered and chaotic. Similarly, Single Page Applications (SPAs) can face a growing challenge – maintaining order within their user interfaces (UIs) as features and functionalities increase.

Here's how UI complexity can become a problem in SPAs:

Spaghetti Code: Without proper organization, the UI code can become tangled and difficult to understand, maintain, and modify. This is akin to having wires, furniture, and decorations all jumbled together in a house – difficult to navigate and update.

Debugging Difficulties: Complex UIs with intertwined logic can make debugging issues a nightmare. Imagine trying to fix a flickering light in your house if the electrical wiring is a mess – it's much harder to pinpoint the problem.

Reduced Maintainability: As the UI grows, making changes or adding new features becomes cumbersome and time-consuming.

Just like renovating a cluttered house is a bigger project than a tidy one, maintaining a complex SPA without clear structure can be a challenge.

This is where Component-Based Design (CBD) comes in to save the day! By applying CBD principles, you can transform your UI from a chaotic mess into a well-organized and manageable space. The next section, 6.2 Core Principles of Component-Based Design, will explore how CBD helps us conquer UI complexity in SPAs.

6.2 The Pillars of Order: Core Principles of Component-Based Design

Chapter 6.1 highlighted the challenges of maintaining complex UIs in SPAs. Thankfully, Component-Based Design (CBD) offers a structured approach to overcome this hurdle. Let's delve into the core principles that underpin CBD:

Single Responsibility Principle:

-Imagine each component in your SPA as a single-purpose appliance in your house. A toaster simply toasts bread, a lamp provides light, and so on. Similarly, the Single Responsibility Principle dictates that each component should have a clear and well-defined responsibility.

-This promotes modularity, where each component focuses on a specific task, making the overall UI easier to understand and maintain. A well-designed toaster wouldn't try to also blend smoothies – that would be a complex and error-prone appliance!

Separation of Concerns:

-This principle emphasizes keeping different aspects of your UI development separate.

-Imagine separating the electrical wiring (data and logic) from the light fixtures (UI representation) in your house. Similarly, in CBD, components typically focus on UI representation (what to display) and delegate logic and data management to separate concerns like application state or business logic.

-This separation improves code organization and reduces the complexity of individual components. You wouldn't expect your light fixture to know how to generate electricity – that's the job of the wiring in the walls!

Composability:

-This principle emphasizes the ability to combine and nest components to create more complex UI structures.

-Imagine building your house room by room, then assembling those rooms together. Similarly, CBD promotes building UIs from smaller, reusable components that can be easily combined to form more intricate layouts. This allows for a flexible and scalable approach to UI development. Just like Lego bricks, well-designed components can be snapped together to create a variety of structures!

By adhering to these core principles, you can develop well-structured, maintainable, and reusable UI components for your ClojureScript SPAs. The next section, 6.3 Building Reusable Components with ClojureScript, will explore practical aspects of creating such components.

6.3 Building Blocks for Orderly UIs: Creating Reusable Components in ClojureScript

Now that we've explored the core principles of Component-Based Design (CBD) in Chapter 6.2, let's delve into practical aspects of building reusable components with ClojureScript. Here are some key considerations:

Props: The Ingredients for Your Components

-Imagine components as recipes, and props are the ingredients. Just like a recipe specifies the ingredients needed for a dish, props provide data to components, allowing them to be flexible and adaptable to different contexts.

-Props are typically immutable data structures like maps or vectors that are passed into component functions.

+By using props, you can create components that can be reused in various parts of your SPA with different data, reducing code duplication and promoting reusability. For example, a button component could accept props like `:label` and `:on-click` to display different text and perform different actions depending on where it's used in your UI.

State Management: Keeping Your Components in Sync

-While some state might be managed within components (e.g., toggling a checkbox), complex UIs often benefit from a separate state management solution.

-In ClojureScript, atoms or libraries like `re-com` or `Om Next` are commonly used for state management. These solutions centralize state updates and ensure consistency across components.

-Imagine your house having a central thermostat to control the temperature throughout, rather than each room having its own independent temperature control – this is analogous to using a centralized state management solution to keep your SPA's UI components in sync.

Event Handling: Responding to User Interactions

-Components can define event handlers to respond to user interactions, like button clicks or form submissions.

-These event handlers are functions that are triggered when the specific event occurs.

-Inside the event handler, you can access the user's input or perform actions based on the interaction. Event handlers make your UI dynamic and interactive, allowing components to react to user input and update accordingly.

-Imagine a light switch component in your house – flipping the switch triggers an event handler (turning the light on or off).

By following these guidelines and leveraging the features of your chosen ClojureScript UI library, you can create well-designed, reusable components that form the building blocks of your SPA's UI. The next section, 6.4 Advanced Component Patterns for Complex UIs, will explore some advanced techniques for managing intricate UI interactions in your SPAs.

6.4 Beyond the Basics: Advanced Component Patterns for intricate UIs

As your ClojureScript SPAs evolve and handle more complex interactions, you might explore these advanced component patterns to manage intricate UI behaviors:

Presentational Components:

-Imagine these components as the facade of your house – they focus solely on how things look.

-Presentational components receive data through props and are responsible for displaying that data in a visually appealing way, but delegate any logic or state management to other components.

-This separation of concerns promotes cleaner and more maintainable code. For example, a product card component might only care about displaying product information (name, price, image) received as props, without handling any logic related to adding the product to a cart or handling discounts.

Container Components:

-Think of container components as the rooms or sections within your house that hold the furniture (presentational components).

-These components manage the state and interactions for a specific section of your UI. They often group presentational components together and handle communication between them.

-Container components might also handle logic related to fetching data or handling user interactions within their section. For example, a shopping cart component might be a container component that holds presentational components for each item in the cart, manages the overall cart state (total price, number of items), and handles interactions like removing items from the cart.

Higher-Order Components (HOCs):

Imagine HOCs as decorators or enhancements for your components.

These are functions that take a component and return a new component, often used to add functionality or behavior to existing components without modifying their original code.

HOCs are a powerful tool for promoting code reusability and reducing code duplication. For example, you might have an HOC that adds authentication logic to any component it's applied to, ensuring only authorized users can access certain parts of your SPA.

By understanding and applying these advanced component patterns, you can structure your SPAs for better organization, maintainability, and scalability. These patterns allow you to create well-defined components with clear responsibilities, leading to a more robust and manageable codebase for complex user interfaces.

The next section, 6.5 Benefits of Component-Based Design: A Recap, will summarize the advantages of using CBD in your ClojureScript SPAs.

6.5 Reaping the Rewards: Benefits of Component-Based Design

Throughout Chapter 6, we've explored Component-Based Design (CBD) as a powerful approach to structuring and maintaining complex UIs in ClojureScript SPAs. Now, let's revisit the key benefits of embracing CBD:

Manageable UIs: By breaking down complex UIs into smaller, reusable components, CBD promotes a more organized structure. This makes your UI easier to reason about, understand, and modify as your SPA grows. Imagine a well-organized house with clearly defined rooms – it's much easier to navigate and maintain compared to a cluttered space.

Improved Developer Experience: A well-structured component-based codebase is like a well-organized toolbox for developers. Components with clear responsibilities and separation of concerns are easier to understand, test, and modify. This leads to a more efficient and productive development experience.

Scalability: As your SPA expands with new features and functionalities, CBD allows you to easily scale your UI. You can create new components or extend existing ones to accommodate the growing needs of your application. Imagine adding a new room to your house – with a well-designed foundation (CBD), you can expand easily without having to rebuild the entire structure.

By adhering to the core principles and utilizing the techniques discussed in this chapter, you can leverage CBD to conquer the challenges of UI complexity and build robust, maintainable, and scalable SPAs in ClojureScript.

Chapter 7:

Styling Your SPA for a Professional Look and Feel

Congratulations! You've mastered the fundamentals of building interactive UIs with ClojureScript components. Now, let's shift our focus to the visual presentation of your SPA. This chapter explores essential concepts and techniques for styling your SPA to achieve a professional and visually appealing look and feel.

7.1 The Power of Looks: Why Styling Matters in Your SPA

Imagine walking into two restaurants with identical menus. One has a messy, cluttered atmosphere, while the other boasts clean lines, modern furniture, and a curated ambiance. Which one would you be more likely to enjoy your meal in? The same logic applies to Single Page Applications (SPAs). While functionality is crucial, visual appeal plays a significant role in user experience (UX) and brand perception.

Here's why styling matters in your SPA:

Enhanced User Experience (UX): A well-styled SPA is more than just visually pleasing. It guides users through the application intuitively. Clear visual cues, like color contrast for buttons or spacing between elements, make the SPA easier to navigate and interact with. Imagine a restaurant with poorly lit menus and unclear signage – it would be frustrating to order food! Effective styling in an SPA is like having a well-organized restaurant layout and clear menus, making the user's experience more enjoyable.

Stronger Brand Identity: Just like a restaurant's decor reflects its brand image, the style of your SPA can reinforce your brand identity. A consistent and professional design language using specific color palettes, fonts, and layouts sets you apart from competitors and creates a recognizable brand experience. For example, a professional service company's SPA might use a clean, minimalist style with muted colors to convey trust and efficiency, while a children's clothing store's SPA might be more playful and colorful to reflect its brand.

By investing in styling your SPA, you're not just making it look better; you're creating a positive user experience and strengthening your brand identity. The next section, 7.2 Popular Styling Approaches for ClojureScript SPAs, will explore different methods to achieve that professional look and feel.

7.2 Popular Avenues to Beautify Your SPA: Styling Approaches in ClojureScript

Chapter 7.1 highlighted the significance of styling in SPAs. Now, let's delve into three common methods to achieve a polished look and feel for your ClojureScript application:

CSS Frameworks:

Bootstrap:

Clojure

```clojure
(defn app []

  [:div {:class "container"}
```

```clojure
    [:h1 {:class "display-4 text-center"} "My
Bootstrap SPA"]

    [:button {:class "btn btn-primary"} "Click
me!"]])
```

This example uses Bootstrap classes like `"container"`, `"display-4"`, and `"btn btn-primary"` to create a basic layout with a heading and button.

Tailwind CSS:

Clojure

```clojure
(defn app []

  [:div {:class "flex justify-center items-center
h-screen"}

        [:h1 {:class "text-3xl font-bold
text-center"} "My Tailwind SPA"]

        [:button {:class "bg-blue-500
hover:bg-blue-700 text-white font-bold py-2 px-4
rounded"}

    "Click me!"]])
```

This example utilizes Tailwind's utility classes like `"flex"`, `"justify-center"`, `"items-center"`, and more to achieve a similar layout with a button.

Materialize:

Clojure

```clojure
(defn app []

  [:div {:class "container center-align"}

      [:h1 {:class "card-title"} "My Materialize
SPA"]

          [:a  {:class  "waves-effect  waves-light
btn-large" :href "#"}

      "Click me!"]])
```

This example uses Materialize classes like `"container"`, `"center-align"`, `"card-title"`, and `"waves-effect waves-light btn-large"` to create a layout with a Material Design-inspired button.

CSS Modules:

Clojure

```clojure
(defn todo-item [todo]
```

```
  [:div {:class (str "todo-item " (:completed
todo))}

  [:span {:class "todo-text"} (:text todo)]

  (when-not (:completed todo)

      [:button {:class "todo-complete-btn"
:on-click #(swap! todo-items update-in [(.id
todo) :completed] not)}

    "Complete"])])


(defmodule todo-item.style

  (.todo-item

    :display "flex"

    :align-items "center"

    :padding "10px")

  (.todo-text

    :flex-grow 1)

  (.todo-complete-btn

    :margin-left "10px"

    :padding "5px"

    :border "none"

    :background-color "#ccc"))
```

This approach promotes style isolation. The `todo-item` component has a corresponding CSS module (`todo-item.style`) where styles are defined using the component name as a prefix to avoid conflicts with styles from other components.

Styled-Components:

Clojure

```clojure
(defn TodoItem [todo]

  [:div {:style {:display "flex"

                 :align-items "center"

                 :padding "10px"}})

   [:span {:style {:flex-grow 1}} (:text todo)]

   (when-not (:completed todo)

     [:button {:style {:margin-left "10px"

                       :padding "5px"

                       :border "none"

                       :background-color "#ccc"}

               :on-click #(swap! todo-items
update-in [(.id todo) :completed] not)}

       "Complete"])])
```

Styled-components allow you to write CSS directly within your ClojureScript components using template literals. Here, styles are defined within the `TodoItem` component itself.

The best approach depends on your project's needs, team preferences, and desired level of customization. Consider factors like the size and complexity of your SPA, your familiarity with different styling techniques, and the importance of a pre-defined design language.

The next section, 7.3 Core Principles of Effective SPA Styling, will explore some general principles to follow regardless of the styling method you choose.

7.3 Core Principles of Effective SPA Styling (with Clojure/examples)

1. Consistency (Using CSS Modules):

Imagine separate CSS modules for different components, ensuring styles are scoped locally.

Clojure

```
(defn todo-item [todo]

    [:div {:class (str "todo-item " (:completed
todo))}

    [:span {:class "todo-text"} (:text todo)]

    (when-not (:completed todo)

        [:button {:class "todo-complete-btn"
:on-click #(swap! todo-items update-in [(.id
todo) :completed] not)}
```

```
        "Complete"])])


(defmodule todo-item.style

  (.todo-item

    :display "flex"

    :align-items "center"

    :padding "10px")

  (.todo-text

    :flex-grow 1)

  (.todo-complete-btn

    :margin-left "10px"

    :padding "5px"

    :border "none"

    :background-color "#ccc"))
```

This example demonstrates a `todo-item` component with a corresponding CSS module (`todo-item.style`). Styles are defined within the module and prefixed with the component name to avoid conflicts.

2. Readability (Font Sizes and Colors):

Clojure

```
(defn app []
```

```clojure
[:div {:style {:font-family "sans-serif"

                :font-size "16px"

                :color "#333"}}

  "Welcome to my SPA!"])
```

This example sets the overall font family, size, and color for the app using inline styles. Alternatively, you can define these styles in a CSS class and apply it to the div element.

3. Responsiveness (Flexbox and Media Queries):

Clojure

```clojure
(defn header []

  [:header {:style {:display "flex"

                    :justify-content "space-between"

                    :padding "10px 20px"}}

   [:h1 "My SPA"]

   [:nav

    [:a {:href "/" :class "nav-link"} "Home"]

      [:a {:href "/about" :class "nav-link"} "About"]]])


(defonce media-queries
```

```clojure
"(@media (max-width: 768px))"

[:.header {:display "block"

           :text-align "center"}}])


(when-not (nil? js/document.querySelector)

  (doseq [query media-queries]

    (.append js/document.querySelector "style"
(domify query))))
```

This example uses flexbox for layout within the `header` component. Additionally, media queries are defined to adjust the layout for smaller screens (less than 768px wide). The `when-not` form ensures the styles are only applied in a browser environment.

7.4 Practical Tips for Styling Your SPA with ClojureScript Examples

Chapter 7.2 explored various approaches to achieve a professional look and feel for your ClojureScript SPA. Now, let's delve into some practical guidance you can implement in your projects:

Leverage Preprocessors (Sass):

Imagine using Sass to create cleaner and more maintainable CSS code.

Clojure

```scss
// todo-item.scss

.todo-item {

  display: flex;

  align-items: center;

  padding: 10px;


  &__text {

    flex-grow: 1;

  }


  &__complete-btn {

    margin-left: 10px;

    padding: 5px;

    border: none;

    background-color: #ccc;

  }

}
```

This example demonstrates using Sass with nesting (`&__`) to organize styles for the `todo-item` component and its sub-elements (`.todo-item__text`,

`.todo-item__complete-btn`). Sass also offers features like variables and mixins for improved code reusability.

Utilize Design Tools (Figma):

Consider using design tools like Figma or Adobe XD to streamline your workflow.

These tools allow you to create mockups and define a style guide that visually represents your SPA's design. This ensures consistency throughout the development process and helps bridge the gap between designers and developers.

Test on Different Devices (Responsive Design):

Responsive design is crucial in today's multi-device world.

Clojure

```clojure
(defn header []

  [:header {:style {:display "flex"

                                  :justify-content
"space-between"

                     :padding "10px 20px"}}

   [:h1 "My SPA"]

   [:nav

    [:a {:href "/" :class "nav-link"} "Home"]

        [:a {:href "/about" :class "nav-link"}
"About"]]])
```

```clojure
(defonce media-queries

  "(@media (max-width: 768px))"

  [:.header {:display "block"

             :text-align "center"}}])


(when-not (nil? js/document.querySelector)

  (doseq [query media-queries]

    (.append js/document.querySelector "style"
(domify query))))
```

This example uses flexbox for layout within the `header` component. Additionally, media queries are defined to adjust the layout for smaller screens (less than 768px wide). The `when-not` form ensures the styles are only applied in a browser environment.

By following these tips and incorporating the provided ClojureScript code snippets, you can enhance your SPA's visual appeal and user experience. Remember to choose the styling approach that best suits your project's requirements and leverage the available tools to streamline your development process.

7.5 Beyond the Basics: Advanced Styling Techniques with ClojureScript Examples

Chapter 7.4 covered practical tips for styling your ClojureScript SPA. Now, we'll delve into more advanced techniques to elevate the visual experience and user interaction:

Animations and Transitions:

-Subtle animations and transitions can improve the user experience by adding a touch of polish and making interactions feel more fluid. Here's an example using the `re-frame` library and CSS for a basic button hover effect:

Clojure

```clojure
(defn button [label on-click]

    [:button   {:class   "my-button"   :on-click
on-click} label])



(defn styles []

  [:.my-button

        {:transition   "background-color   0.2s
ease-in-out"}

   {:background-color "#ddd"}

   [:hover {:background-color "#ccc"}]])



(reg-fx :styles styles)
```

This example defines a `button` component that triggers an `on-click` event. The `styles` function defines a CSS class for the button with a transition effect for background color on hover. The `reg-fx` function from `re-frame` registers this stylesheet to be included in the application.

Microinteractions:

Microinteractions are small, interactive elements that enhance user engagement and provide valuable feedback within your SPA. Here's an example using CSS for a simple toggle switch:

Clojure

```clojure
(defn toggle [checked on-toggle]

  [:label {:class "toggle-switch"}

    [:input {:type "checkbox" :checked checked
:on-change #(on-toggle (not checked))}]

    [:span {:class (str "toggle-slider " (if
checked "active" ""))}]]])


(defn styles []

  [:.toggle-switch

  {:display "inline-block"

   :position "relative"

   :width "60px"
```

```
      :height "34px"}

   [:input {:opacity 0

              :width "0"

              :height "0"}]]
  [:.toggle-slider

   {:position "absolute"

    :cursor "pointer"

    :top "0"

    :left "0"

    :right "0"

    :bottom "0"

    :background-color "#ccc"

    :transition ".4s ease-all"}

      [:.toggle-slider.active {:background-color
"#3498db"}]])


(reg-fx :styles styles)
```

This example defines a `toggle` component that renders a checkbox styled as a toggle switch. The `styles` function defines the styles for the toggle element, including the slider that visually represents the checked state.

Accessibility:

Ensuring your SPA adheres to accessibility guidelines (WCAG) is crucial for making it usable by everyone, regardless of their abilities. Here are some general tips:

-Use semantic HTML elements to convey the meaning of content (headings, buttons, forms).

-Provide clear and concise labels for interactive elements.

-Ensure adequate color contrast for text and interactive elements.

-Use keyboard navigation to allow users to interact with the SPA without a mouse.

While these tips don't involve specific ClojureScript code, they are essential considerations for responsible SPA development. Several libraries like `accessible-remix` can assist with implementing accessibility features in your ClojureScript projects.

By incorporating these advanced techniques, you can create a more visually engaging and user-friendly SPA. Remember to prioritize accessibility to ensure everyone can benefit from your application.

Chapter 8:

Taking Your SPA to the Next Level: Authentication and Authorization

Congratulations! You've mastered the fundamentals of building interactive and visually appealing SPAs with ClojureScript. Now, it's time to delve into securing your application by implementing authentication and authorization mechanisms. This chapter explores strategies to manage user access and protect your SPA's data.

8.1 The Guardians of Your SPA: Authentication and Authorization

Imagine a social media app where anyone could edit anyone else's profile – chaos, right? Authentication and authorization are the cornerstones of security in SPAs that handle sensitive data or require user login for specific features. They work together to ensure only the right people have access to the right things within your application.

Authentication:

-Acts as the gatekeeper, verifying a user's identity. This typically involves confirming a username and password combination or leveraging existing providers like Google or Facebook. Imagine a high-security building – authentication checks your ID and credentials before granting entry.

Authorization:

-Determines the level of access a logged-in user has within the SPA. Like a security clearance level, it dictates what actions a user can perform. For instance, an authorized editor might be able to modify blog posts, while a viewer might only be able to read them.

By implementing these mechanisms, you achieve several benefits:

Protect sensitive user data: Authentication ensures only authorized users can access confidential information.

Control access to functionalities: Authorization restricts actions based on user roles, preventing unauthorized edits or actions.

Enhance trust and security: Robust authentication and authorization build user confidence in the security of your SPA.

In essence, authentication verifies "who you are," while authorization determines "what you can do" within your SPA. The next section, 8.2 Authentication Approaches for ClojureScript SPAs, will delve into different methods for handling user authentication.

8.2 Securing Your SPA: Authentication Approaches in ClojureScript

Chapter 8.1 highlighted the importance of authentication and authorization in SPAs. Now, let's explore various methods to implement authentication in your ClojureScript application:

Server-Side Authentication:

-This traditional approach involves your ClojureScript SPA communicating with a server-side application (often written in Clojure) to handle authentication logic. Here's a simplified workflow:

-The user submits their login credentials (username and password) through the SPA.

-The SPA sends the credentials to the server-side application in a secure manner (e.g., POST request with HTTPS).

-The server-side application validates the credentials against a user database or other authentication source.

-If the credentials are valid, the server generates an authentication token (e.g., session ID or JWT) and sends it back to the SPA.

-The SPA stores the token securely (e.g., HttpOnly cookies) and includes it in subsequent requests to the server for verification.

-This approach offers fine-grained control over the authentication process but requires additional server-side development.

Client-Side Authentication with Providers:

-This method leverages existing authentication providers like Google, Facebook, or OAuth for user login. Here's the general flow:

-The user initiates login through a provider's button or widget within the SPA.

-The user is redirected to the provider's login page to authenticate.

-Upon successful login, the provider redirects the user back to the SPA with an authentication token or code.

-The SPA uses this token or code to exchange for user information or an access token from the provider's API.

-The SPA can then use the access token to verify the user's identity with the provider and grant access to SPA functionalities.

This approach simplifies setup but introduces reliance on external services and their APIs.

Token-Based Authentication:

A popular approach for RESTful APIs. Here's a typical scenario:

-The user logs in through the SPA, and the server-side application validates the credentials.

-If successful, the server issues a token (often a JSON Web Token or JWT) to the SPA.

-The SPA stores the token securely (e.g., HttpOnly cookies) and includes it in the authorization header of subsequent requests to access protected resources on the server.

-The server verifies the validity of the token before granting access to the requested resources.

-This approach is flexible but necessitates careful token management on both the client and server sides.

Choosing the best approach depends on your project's requirements. Server-side authentication offers more control but requires more development effort. Client-side authentication with providers is simpler to set up but might introduce external dependencies. Token-based authentication is flexible but demands robust token management strategies.

The next section, 8.3 Implementing Authentication in a ClojureScript SPA, will provide a simplified example of server-side authentication in ClojureScript.

8.3 Putting Authentication into Action: A ClojureScript Example

Chapter 8.2 explored various authentication approaches for ClojureScript SPAs. Now, let's delve into a basic server-side authentication implementation using ClojureScript and Clojure. Remember, this is a simplified example for illustrative purposes. In a real-world application, you'd likely use a more secure storage mechanism for tokens (e.g., HttpOnly cookies) and implement additional security measures.

ClojureScript (SPA):

Clojure

```
(defn login [username password]

  (.fetch "/api/login" {:method "POST"

                        :body (js/JSON.stringify
{:username username :password password})

                        :headers {"Content-Type"
"application/json"}}))


(defn handle-login-response [response]

  (if (= (:status response) 200)
```

```clojure
(do

        (let [token (-> response js/json (.get
"token"))]

            (.localStorage js/window setItem
"auth_token" token)))

    (js/console.error "Login failed!")))
```

This code defines a `login` function that sends a POST request to the server-side API endpoint `/api/login` with the username and password in the request body. The `handle-login-response` function processes the response. If successful (status code 200), it extracts the token from the JSON response and stores it in the browser's localStorage (not recommended for production due to security concerns).

Server-Side (Clojure):

Clojure

```clojure
(defn login-handler [request]

  (let [login-params (request-parameters request)

        username (:username login-params)

        password (:password login-params)]

    (if (valid-credentials? username password)

      {:status 200

          :body {:token "your_secure_token"}}    ;
Replace with actual token generation
```

```
{:status 401 ; Unauthorized

      :body {:message "Invalid username or
password"}}))))
```

This Clojure code defines a `login-handler` function that handles login requests. It retrieves the username and password from the request parameters and calls a hypothetical `valid-credentials?` function to verify them (replace this with your actual user authentication logic). If valid, the handler returns a response with a status code of 200 and a body containing a token (replace `"your_secure_token"` with your token generation mechanism). Otherwise, it returns a 401 Unauthorized status code and an error message.

Important Considerations:

-This example uses localStorage for demonstration purposes only. In a production application, you'd likely use HttpOnly cookies for more secure token storage.

-Implement robust password hashing and salting on the server-side to protect user credentials.

-Consider using a library like `secretary` for managing application routes and authorization checks on the SPA side.

-Always validate and sanitize user input to prevent security vulnerabilities like XSS (Cross-Site Scripting).

Remember, authentication is a crucial security component. While this example provides a basic structure, ensure you follow best practices and secure coding principles when implementing authentication in your ClojureScript SPAs.

The next section, 8.4 Authorization: Controlling User Access, will explore how to manage user permissions within your SPA after successful authentication.

8.4 Authorization: Controlling User Access

Now that you've explored authentication methods in Chapter 8.3, let's delve into authorization in Chapter 8.4. Authorization determines what actions a logged-in user can perform within your ClojureScript SPA.

8.4.1 Understanding Authorization

Imagine a library with different sections – the children's section allows browsing picture books, while the restricted section requires authorization (like a library card) to access research materials. Authorization in SPAs functions similarly:

-It determines a user's access level based on their role (e.g., admin, editor, viewer).

-It dictates what actions a user can perform within the SPA (e.g., editing posts, deleting comments).

8.4.2 Common Authorization Strategies

Here are some widely used authorization strategies:

Role-Based Access Control (RBAC):

-A popular approach that assigns users to predefined roles (e.g., admin, editor, viewer) with associated permissions.

-The SPA checks a user's role upon login and grants access based on the assigned permissions.

-For instance, an admin might have permission to edit all content, while an editor might only edit specific sections.

Attribute-Based Access Control (ABAC):

-A more granular approach that considers various attributes besides roles when making authorization decisions.

-These attributes can include user location, device type, time of day, or specific data sensitivity.

-ABAC offers more flexibility but can be more complex to implement.

Resource-Based Access Control (RBAC):

-Focuses on controlling access to specific resources within the SPA (e.g., individual files, database records).

-Permissions are defined for each resource, and users are granted access based on their roles or attributes.

The best approach depends on your application's needs. RBAC is a good starting point for many SPAs, while ABAC or RBAC might be suitable for scenarios requiring more fine-grained control.

8.4.3 Implementing Authorization in a ClojureScript SPA

Here's a general outline for implementing authorization in a ClojureScript SPA (specific implementation will vary based on your chosen approach):

Store User Roles or Permissions:

-Upon successful authentication, store the user's role or permission information in the SPA's state or local storage (securely!).

Protect Routes and Components:

-Use libraries like `secretary` to manage application routes.

-Wrap protected routes or components with authorization checks. These checks can compare the user's role or permissions against the required access level for the specific route or component.

Handle Unauthorized Access Attempts:

-If a user tries to access a protected resource without proper authorization, gracefully handle the situation.

-You can redirect them to a login page or display an error message indicating insufficient permissions.

8.4.4 Additional Considerations

-Securely store user roles or permissions. Avoid storing sensitive information directly in the client-side code.

-Consider using authorization libraries or frameworks that can simplify authorization logic management.

-Regularly review and update your authorization policies to ensure they align with your application's evolving needs.

By effectively implementing authorization, you can create a secure and controlled environment within your ClojureScript SPA, ensuring users can only access the functionalities and data they are authorized to.

This concludes Chapter 8: Taking Your SPA to the Next Level: Authentication and Authorization. By understanding and implementing these concepts, you can build robust and secure SPAs that protect user data and provide a seamless user experience.

Chapter 9:

Testing and Debugging Your ClojureScript SPA for Confidence

Congratulations! You've mastered the fundamentals of building interactive, visually appealing, and secure ClojureScript SPAs. Now, it's time to ensure your creation functions as intended. This chapter explores strategies for testing and debugging your SPA, empowering you to deliver high-quality applications with confidence.

9.1 The Importance of Testing in Single-Page Applications (SPAs)

Imagine launching a beautiful SPA, only to find it riddled with bugs that frustrate users. Testing is the shield that protects your SPA from such pitfalls. Let's explore why testing is crucial for SPAs:

Unveiling Bugs Early: Testing helps identify errors and malfunctions during development, preventing them from reaching production and causing user problems.

Ensuring Expected Behavior: Through testing, you verify that your SPA functions as intended across various scenarios and user interactions. It's like checking if all the features work as designed under different conditions.

Enhancing Code Quality: The process of testing encourages you to write clean, maintainable, and well-documented code. Think of it as refining your code for clarity and better organization.

Building Developer Confidence: Knowing your SPA is well-tested gives you peace of mind. You can focus on new features and improvements without worrying about hidden bugs lurking in the codebase.

In essence, testing acts as a quality assurance measure for SPAs. It safeguards the user experience, improves development practices, and instills confidence in your work. The next section, 9.2 Testing Approaches for ClojureScript SPAs, will delve into different testing methods you can employ for your ClojureScript applications.

9.2 Guarding Your SPA: Testing Strategies for ClojureScript

Chapter 9.1 highlighted the significance of testing in SPAs. Now, let's delve into specific testing approaches you can leverage to ensure the quality and robustness of your ClojureScript SPAs:

Unit Testing: The Building Block Guardian

-Unit testing focuses on isolating and testing individual components or functions within your SPA. It's like meticulously examining each building block to ensure it functions as expected.

-Frameworks like `test.js` or `cljs-test` are popular choices for writing unit tests in ClojureScript. These frameworks allow you to create test cases that provide specific inputs to your components or functions and verify the expected outputs.

-By effectively implementing unit tests, you can guarantee that the fundamental building blocks of your SPA work correctly, laying a solid foundation for the entire application.

Integration Testing: Ensuring Component Harmony

-Integration testing goes beyond individual components. It examines how different components interact and work together. Imagine testing how gears in a machine mesh – that's the essence of integration testing.

-You can simulate user interactions or component communication to verify that the overall system behaves as intended when various components collaborate.

-Tools like `domina` (for DOM manipulation) or `phantomjs` (a headless browser) can be useful for simulating browser environments and testing how components interact with each other.

-Integration tests provide assurance that your SPA's components function cohesively to deliver the desired user experience.

End-to-End (E2E) Testing: The User in the Driver's Seat

-E2E testing simulates real user interactions with your entire SPA through a browser. It's like having a user virtually test drive your application.

-Frameworks like `Selenium` or `Nightwatch.js` can be used to automate browser interactions and verify the SPA's overall functionality from a user's perspective.

-E2E tests provide a high-level view of how users will experience your SPA, ensuring it functions seamlessly from start to finish.

Manual Testing: The Human Touch

-While automated testing is essential, manual testing remains valuable. It allows you to explore the SPA from a user's standpoint and identify usability issues or edge cases that automated tests might miss.

-Think of manual testing as putting yourself in the user's shoes and navigating the SPA to discover any potential irregularities in the user experience.

The Right Approach: A Testing Blend

The most effective testing strategy often combines these methods. Unit tests provide a safety net for individual components, integration tests ensure components work together, E2E tests validate overall functionality, and manual testing refines the user experience. By using a combination of these approaches, you can establish a robust testing suite that safeguards the quality of your ClojureScript SPAs.

The next section, 9.3 Debugging Techniques for ClojureScript, will explore methods to troubleshoot issues that might arise during development.

9.3 Conquering Challenges: Debugging Techniques for ClojureScript

Even with a comprehensive testing suite, encountering bugs is inevitable during SPA development. Fortunately, various debugging techniques can help you identify and fix these issues in your ClojureScript SPAs.

Browser Developer Tools: Your Inspection Arsenal

Modern browsers come equipped with built-in developer tools that are vital for debugging SPAs. These tools act as your inspection gadgets to examine your application's inner workings.

Utilize the console to:

-Inspect variables and their values at any point in your code.

-Log messages to track the flow of execution and identify errors.

-Set breakpoints to pause execution at specific lines of code, allowing you to examine the application's state at that point.

-The network tab can help diagnose issues with API calls or resource loading. If your SPA isn't fetching data as expected, the network tab can provide clues.

REPL (Read-Eval-Print Loop): A Playground for Exploration

The REPL is a powerful tool for interactive development in ClojureScript. Think of it as a code playground where you can experiment and test ideas.

You can leverage the REPL to:

-Evaluate expressions and test functions directly within the browser environment. This allows you to try out small pieces of code and observe their behavior.

-Inspect data structures and their contents to ensure they hold the expected values.

The REPL provides a way to iteratively test and debug your SPA's logic in a more interactive manner.

Logging and Debugging Libraries: Powerful Allies

Consider using libraries like `clojure-debugger` or `figwheel` to enhance your debugging experience. These libraries provide additional features that can streamline the debugging process.

Some of the benefits these libraries offer include:

-Source code mapping: This allows you to see the original ClojureScript code corresponding to the generated JavaScript, making debugging more intuitive.

-Stack traces: When errors occur, stack traces pinpoint the exact location in your code where the error originated, aiding in identifying the root cause.

-Hot reloading: This feature allows you to make code changes and see them reflected in the browser without a full page refresh, accelerating the debugging cycle.

Debugging Mindset: A Systematic Approach

When approaching debugging, adopt a systematic and logical mindset. Think of it like solving a puzzle.

Break down the problem into smaller, more manageable steps:

-Isolate the issue: Try to pinpoint the specific area of your code where the unexpected behavior occurs.

-Experiment with potential solutions: Once you've isolated the issue, make incremental code changes and observe their effects.

-Utilize debugging tools: Leverage the browser developer tools, REPL, and debugging libraries to aid in your investigation.

-Seek help if needed: Don't hesitate to consult online resources, communities, or fellow developers if you get stuck.

By following these techniques and cultivating a systematic debugging approach, you'll be well-equipped to troubleshoot issues and ensure the smooth operation of your ClojureScript SPAs.

The next section, 9.4 Additional Tips for Testing and Debugging, provides some helpful pointers to consider as you embark on your testing and debugging journey.

9.4 Additional Tips for Testing and Debugging

Write testable code: Structure your code in a way that facilitates unit testing. This means favoring pure functions with clear inputs and outputs. Components that rely on external factors or side effects can be trickier to test in isolation, so try to design your components with testability in mind.

Test early and often: Integrate testing into your development workflow from the beginning. Don't wait until the end of development to start testing – the sooner you catch bugs, the easier they are to fix.

Automate repetitive tasks: Use automated testing tools to streamline the testing process. This can save you time and effort in the long run, and it can help ensure that your SPA is thoroughly tested before each deployment.

Document your tests: Clear and concise test descriptions enhance the maintainability of your codebase and foster collaboration with other developers. If someone else needs to understand or modify your tests, well-documented tests will make that process much easier.

Seek feedback: Involve others in testing your SPA. Usability testing with real users can help you identify potential issues that you might have missed otherwise. Getting feedback from other developers can also help you ensure that your code is well-written and maintainable.

By following these tips, you can establish a robust testing and debugging culture that will help you deliver high-quality ClojureScript SPAs. Remember, testing is an ongoing process, and it's important to continuously refine your approach as your application evolves.

Chapter 10:

Deploying Your Masterpiece: Sharing Your ClojureScript SPA with the World

Congratulations! You've meticulously crafted a beautiful, interactive, and secure ClojureScript SPA. Now it's time to unleash it upon the world! This chapter explores various deployment strategies to host your SPA and make it accessible to users.

10.1 Choosing a Deployment Strategy

Selecting the Right Deployment Path for Your ClojureScript SPA

After investing time and effort into meticulously crafting your ClojureScript SPA, it's essential to select the most suitable deployment strategy to share it with the world. This decision hinges on several factors:

-Project Requirements: Consider the application's complexity, scalability needs, and performance requirements.

-SEO (Search Engine Optimization) Importance: Does high search engine ranking play a significant role for your SPA?

-Team Expertise: What deployment tools and platforms are your team familiar and comfortable with?

Here's a closer look at some popular deployment strategies for ClojureScript SPAs:

Static File Hosting:

-A straightforward and widely used approach for SPAs built with ClojureScript.

-Platforms like Netlify, Firebase Hosting, or Amazon S3 excel at hosting your SPA's compiled JavaScript, CSS, and HTML files. These platforms are known for their ease of use and affordability.

-If your SPA interacts with a server-side component (like a Clojure backend), you'll need to deploy that separately.

Server-Side Rendering (SSR):

This approach involves rendering your SPA's initial HTML on the server before sending it to the client (user's browser).

This method offers several advantages:

-Enhanced SEO: Search engines can more easily crawl and index your SPA's content, potentially improving search ranking.

-Faster Initial Load Times: Users might experience a quicker initial page load as the server delivers the pre-rendered HTML.

Frameworks like Clojurescript SSR or frameworks like Next.js (with ClojureScript integration) can streamline the SSR implementation for your ClojureScript SPA.

Single-Page Application (SPA) Frameworks:

-If you're leveraging a popular SPA framework like React, Angular, or Vue.js with ClojureScript, these frameworks often provide built-in deployment mechanisms or tools.

-These frameworks often streamline the build process and offer seamless deployment to various hosting platforms. Consult your chosen framework's documentation for specific guidance.

Choosing the Best Fit

The optimal deployment strategy depends on your project's specific requirements and your team's preferences. For instance, if SEO is a top priority and you have experience with SSR, that might be a compelling choice. On the other hand, if you have a simpler SPA and prefer a straightforward approach, static file hosting might be perfectly suitable.

By carefully considering these factors and deployment options, you can select the strategy that best positions your ClojureScript SPA for success in the real world!

10.2 Benefits of a CI Pipeline for ClojureScript SPAs

Imagine a world where you don't have to worry about manually building, testing, and deploying your ClojureScript SPA every time you make a code change. That's the magic of CI! Here's why incorporating a CI pipeline is beneficial:

Reduced Errors: By automating builds and tests, you can catch errors early in the development process. This helps prevent bugs from creeping into production and frustrating your users.

Faster Deployments: CI pipelines can automate deployments, saving you time and effort. With every code change, the CI pipeline can automatically trigger a build, test, and deployment process, expediting the release cycle.

Improved Consistency: Automation ensures consistency across deployments. There's less chance of human error introducing issues during the build or deployment process.

Setting Up a CI Pipeline with Travis CI

Travis CI is a popular platform for setting up CI pipelines for various projects, including ClojureScript SPAs. Here's a simplified outline to get you started (refer to Travis CI's documentation for detailed instructions):

-Create a Travis CI Account: Sign up for a free or paid Travis CI account depending on your needs.

-Connect Your Project Repository: Link your ClojureScript project's Git repository (e.g., GitHub, GitLab) to Travis CI.

-Create a `.travis.yml` **File:** In your project's root directory, create a YAML file named `.travis.yml`. This file specifies the build instructions and commands that Travis CI will execute.

Here's a basic example `.travis.yml` configuration for a ClojureScript SPA project:

```yaml
YAML

language: clojure

script:

  # Compile your ClojureScript project

  lein deps

  lein cljs build optimized
```

```
# Run your tests (replace with your actual test
command)

lein test
```

This configuration specifies that Travis CI should use Clojure and execute the following commands in the build process:

`lein deps`: Downloads and installs project dependencies.

`lein cljs build optimized`: Compiles your ClojureScript code into optimized JavaScript.

`lein test` (replace with your actual test command): Runs your unit tests.

Beyond the Basics

The `.travis.yml` file allows for more customization. You can define stages for different build steps, deploy scripts for specific platforms, and configure notifications for build failures. Explore Travis CI's documentation to unlock the full potential of CI pipelines for your ClojureScript SPA development.

Remember, CI pipelines are just one tool in your development toolbox. By leveraging CI and other best practices, you can ensure your ClojureScript SPAs are built, tested, and deployed efficiently and reliably.

10.3 Speeding Up Your SPA: The Power of Content Delivery Networks (CDNs)

Imagine users across the globe accessing your ClojureScript SPA. Ideally, everyone should experience a snappy and responsive application. This is where CDNs come in!

-A CDN is a geographically distributed network of servers that cache static content (like JavaScript, CSS, and image files) for your SPA.

-When a user requests your SPA, the CDN delivers the static content from the server closest to the user's location. This significantly reduces latency (delay) compared to fetching content from your origin server (where your SPA resides).

Benefits of Using a CDN for Your ClojureScript SPA:

Improved Load Times: Faster content delivery translates to a quicker initial load time for users, enhancing the overall user experience.

Reduced Server Load: By offloading static content delivery to the CDN, you lessen the burden on your origin server, improving scalability and potentially reducing costs.

Enhanced Availability: CDNs are geographically distributed, so if one server experiences an outage, others can still deliver content, improving the overall reliability of your SPA.

Popular CDN Providers:

Several cloud platforms offer CDN services. Here are some of the most popular options:

- Amazon CloudFront
- Cloudflare
- Google Cloud CDN

Setting Up a CDN

The specific steps for setting up a CDN will vary depending on the provider you choose. However, the general process involves:

Creating a CDN Account: Sign up for an account with your chosen CDN provider.

Adding Your Content: Upload your SPA's static files (JavaScript, CSS, images) to the CDN's storage.

Configuring Your Domain: Map your domain name or subdomain to the CDN's servers to ensure users access content through the CDN.

Updating Your SPA Code: Modify your SPA's code to reference static content from the CDN's URLs instead of your origin server's URLs.

Additional Considerations:

- **Cache invalidation:** Establish a strategy for keeping the CDN's cache fresh when you update your static content.
- **Security:** Ensure your CDN is configured to deliver content securely using HTTPS.

By implementing a CDN, you can take your ClojureScript SPA's performance to the next level, providing a faster and more responsive user experience for a global audience.

10.4 Keeping Your ClojureScript SPA Thriving: Monitoring and Maintenance

Congratulations! You've successfully deployed your ClojureScript SPA and it's live for the world to use. But your work isn't quite finished. Proactive monitoring and maintenance are essential to guarantee a performant, secure, and up-to-date user experience.

Monitoring Practices:

Error Monitoring:

-Implement error monitoring tools to track and address errors that occur in your deployed SPA. These tools can pinpoint issues like JavaScript exceptions or failed API calls.

-By promptly addressing errors, you can prevent them from frustrating your users and ensure a smooth user experience.

Performance Monitoring:

-Keep an eye on key performance metrics like load times, resource usage, and frame rates. Tools like Google Analytics or browser developer tools can provide valuable insights.

-By identifying performance bottlenecks, you can optimize your SPA's code and improve its overall responsiveness.

Analytics:

-Utilize analytics tools to understand how users interact with your SPA. Track metrics like user behavior, feature usage, and conversion rates.

-These analytics provide valuable data for making informed decisions about future improvements and enhancements to your SPA.

Maintenance Practices:

Security Updates:

-Stay informed about security vulnerabilities in the libraries and dependencies used in your SPA. Regularly update these dependencies to address potential security risks.

-Proactive security maintenance safeguards your SPA from exploits and protects user data.

Bug Fixes:

-Address any bugs reported by users or identified through monitoring. Attending to bug fixes promptly enhances the overall quality and usability of your SPA.

New Feature Implementation:

-As your SPA evolves and user needs change, consider implementing new features to improve functionality or address user feedback.

-Continuously iterate and refine your SPA to keep it engaging and valuable for your users.

By following these monitoring and maintenance practices, you can ensure your ClojureScript SPA remains performant, secure, and up-to-date. Remember, a well-maintained SPA not only functions smoothly but also fosters trust and loyalty with your users.

10.5 Domain Name:

-Consider registering a custom domain name (e.g., yourcompany.com) for your SPA instead of relying on a subdomain provided by your hosting platform. A custom domain name enhances your SPA's branding and professionalism, making it more memorable for users. It also provides a more polished user experience.

HTTPS:

-Ensure your SPA uses HTTPS (Hypertext Transfer Protocol Secure) for communication between the browser and the server. HTTPS encrypts data transmission, safeguarding sensitive user information like login credentials or form data. In today's web security landscape, HTTPS is practically mandatory to instill user trust and confidence.

Offline Support (Optional):

-Explore options for providing basic functionality in your SPA even when users are offline. This can be particularly valuable for users with unreliable internet connections or those who may want to access certain features while on the go. For instance, you could enable users to browse cached content or utilize local storage mechanisms.

By incorporating these additional considerations, you can further refine the deployment of your ClojureScript SPA, making it not only functional but also user-friendly, secure, and professional.

www.ingramcontent.com/pod-product-compliance
Lightning Source LLC
LaVergne TN
LVHW051739050326
832903LV00023B/998